introduction

"There is yet more truth and light to break forth from God's Holy Word."

These words were spoken by Pastor John Robinson to the 17th century Pilgrims as they departed from Holland for what would become Massachusetts Bay Colony. God's word is alive. God will always have something new to say to us. So listen up! Because God is still speaking.

There have been and are many Bible studies, and many fine ones. How is a *Listen Up!* Bible study different from another Bible study?

The answer is at once simple and complex. It is simple because the primary point of participation in these Bible studies is to hear God speak to us today. Simple: the point is to hear God speak to us.

But that is also complex, because there is no simple formula that insures this will happen. Hearing God speak is a gift of the Holy Spirit, who is active in our midst. We hope that the background, questions and guides for sharing in these Bible studies will assist you in hearing God speak to us today.

My own experience is that hearing God speak often means having a particular word or phrase or image reach out and grab me or "speak to me" in a way that is deep and real. I may not fully understand why. But some word or phrase—whether from the Bible itself or from our reflection together on it—connects. Perhaps it challenges. It may even "convict," that is reveals a way in which I haven't been honest with myself. Maybe it comforts.

Keep the simple point in mind: our primary purpose is to listen and hear God speak. That also means that it is not our primary purpose to teach you all about the Bible or all about a particular book of the Bible. To be sure, we hope that together we will learn a great deal about whatever book of Scripture is our focus. But the primary purpose is not simply learning information about the Bible. It is hearing God speak. There is a difference.

To this end, this and the other Bible studies in this series encourage you to listen: 1) to the biblical text, 2) to your own questions and responses to it, and 3) to the honest sharing among the participants in your group. Trusting in the power of the Holy Spirit, we believe that in that mix of biblical text, personal engagement, and honest speaking and listening in a respectful group, God's word may be heard.

One of our forebears in the faith, John Calvin, described God's Word as not simply words on a page, but as an event. Calvin said something like this: "God's Word occurs when the same Spirit is present to those who read as to those who wrote." God's Word is an event, an event that happens when receptive hearts and minds open themselves to Scripture in the company of other seekers and believers.

We do hope that you learn something—perhaps a great deal—about the particular book of the Bible that is the topic of this study. But most of all, we hope that this series of lessons and small group suggestions will enable you to hear God speaking words of challenge and words of comfort to you and your companions in this experience.

why 2 corinthians?

ANTHONY B. ROBINSON

In the introduction to our 1 Corinthians Bible Study (which it might be useful to review now), I told a story about being called to my first congregation and finding it to be as divided and factionalized as the U. S. Congress. I more or less stumbled—or was guided—into a strategy of congregation-wide engagement with 1 Corinthians. This proved excellent medicine for the soul of our squabbling church.

Another thing happened not long after I arrived at that church. I got a call from the Baptist minister in town who was quite excited about an upcoming event. A professional football player, a member of the Seattle Seahawks, was going to visit our little hamlet outside of Seattle to make a witness for Christ. "This will be great," said my fellow pastor. "Be sure to bring your youth. When they hear this All-Pro linebacker talk about Jesus, they'll be impressed."

I didn't immediately share this other minister's enthusiasm, though I wasn't quite sure why. And I actually felt a little guilty about not being so fired up about this "great opportunity for evangelism." As I tried to make sense of my hesitation, Paul's Second Letter to the Corinthians helped.

While 1 Corinthians is Paul's counsel to a factionalized congregation, 2 Corinthians is his reflection on what it means to be a minister of the gospel and to lead a congregation—especially when that congregation is itself confused about the meaning of the Christian faith and subject to misleading versions of it.

What does this have to do with the pro football player and his witness for Jesus?

In 2 Corinthians Paul responds to criticism of his preaching and teaching, as well as his leadership. At least some in Corinth were more impressed by other preachers and teachers who pointed early and often to their own incredible spiritual experiences as well as their growing personal star power. The implication of their witness might be summed up as, "Believe in Jesus and your life will be blessed with power, fame and fortune—like mine."

In 2 Corinthians Paul refers to these orators who so impressed the Corinthians as "super-apostles." Paul spoke of himself in less glowing terms. Moreover, he recounted not his achievements, but his struggles and even his failures. Why? Because he believed that talking about one's glowing resumé or achievements subtly shifted the focus. It turned faith into an instrument of personal success and achievement, a means not an end. In doing so the focus was shifted: from God to ourselves. But as Paul wrote in a famous verse from this letter, "We do not proclaim ourselves; we proclaim Jesus Christ as Lord and ourselves as your slaves for Jesus' sake." (4:5)

I think my hesitation about promoting the pro football player's talk was similar to Paul's problem with the "super-apostles" who impressed so many in Corinth. The implication was that something as culturally significant as professional football conferred credibility on the gospel. But in doing so, it risked turning the gospel into another tool of and for our own ego. Paul wasn't, however, preaching "Touchdown Jesus," but "Christ crucified." (Just for the record, I played football and like the sport.)

These issues are still very much with us today, perhaps even more than they were thirty plus years ago when I was a young pastor. Today we have many "celebrity preachers," stars in the religious and spiritual firmament, whose ability to entertain and inspire attracts huge followings and builds "mega-churches." But the questions persist—is it the gospel of Christ crucified that they preach or some other gospel? And is this way of leading a congregation sound? Or do personality-focused ministries fail us, and the church, in the end?

So in 2 Corinthians Paul takes on some of the toughest questions. What is the nature of pastoral ministry? What is the gospel we preach? What is the nature of a minister's authority? And what does it mean to be a leader and to exercise leadership faithfully and well? These are urgent questions today.

Of 2 Corinthians Bible scholar Eugene Peterson wrote, "Paul, studying Jesus, had learned a kind of leadership in which he managed to stay out of the way so that others could deal with God without having to go through him. All who are called to exercise leadership in whatever capacity— parent or coach, pastor or president, teacher or manager—can be grateful to Paul for this letter and to the Corinthians for provoking it."

May we, as we explore this letter together, also know such gratitude.

a brief overview of 2 corinthians

and resources for further study

2 Corinthians is a little choppy, perhaps because it is in all likelihood the compilation of a couple of letters and not just one. Still, it is possible to outline its structure and contents briefly as follows:

Chapters 1–2:13: These chapters might be thought of as "Unfinished Business" as Paul explains why he hasn't visited Corinth as promised and what this means.

Chapters 2:14–Chapter 7: Paul's ministry among the Corinthians—how he understands his role, the gospel and leadership.

Chapters 8–9: The Collection for the Church in Jerusalem (some things here that are particularly useful for stewardship season!)

Chapters 10–13: Paul takes on the "super-apostles" boasting, paradoxically, of his own weaknesses.

If you are interested in a resource for further or more detailed study of 2 Corinthians we suggest Ernest Best's commentary, *Second Corinthians*, in the Interpretation series, John Knox/ Westminster Press, 1987.

lesson 1

The Great Unveiling

2 CORINTHIANS 3:1–18

HOMEWORK

STEP ❶: First Reading

Find a comfortable place to sit, when you can be undisturbed for 15 minutes or so. Read the text slowly, prayerfully and meditatively. Savor the words. Pray them. Put yourself into the text with your sense. What do you hear, smell, or feel? Pay attention to the words or phrases that "speak to you," or "jump out at you." Consider reading it aloud.

STEP ❷: Second Reading

This may happen at the same time as the first reading or at a different time or on another day. For this second reading, note any questions you might have. Is the reading all one, or can you see subsections or parts? Who are the main characters? Is there a plot or story? Note additional information you need—place names, monetary values, etc.—to better understand what's going on.

YOUR NOTES:

STEP ❸: Interpreting the Text

The overall theme of this chapter may be this: the gospel of Jesus Christ brings newness, even *is* newness. Things are no longer the same-old-same-old. Moreover, we apostles of Jesus don't operate according to the usual conventions. The veil that had kept things hidden and kept God and humanity at a distance has been lifted.

These themes unfold in a chapter that has three main parts. In the first, verses 1–3, the governing image is that of the letter of commendation. Remember that in Greco-Roman culture traveling orators and preachers were common. The most well-known of these were that culture's rock stars. In order to introduce themselves and get an audience, these traveling orators/ preachers often carried with them letters of introduction and commendation from influential people, from other towns, or from previous clients. Such letters were probably a combination resumé, reference, plus a little "Who's Who" type listing thrown in. Relying on these letters of commendation was standard operating procedure, used by the orators and preachers that the Corinthians preferred to Paul. Perhaps they had asked him, "Where are your letters of reference? Where are your endorsements?"

Paul's answer was, "You are my letter of commendation. You," he said, "are a 'letter of Christ.'" What counts, argued Paul, was not his *curriculum vitae* or his list of honorary degrees. What counted was the community he had served as founding pastor. Their life is the most important testimony to, and evidence of, his ministry.

Sometimes today, people are impressed—as were the Corinthians—by gaudy claims of achievement made by clergy. They may boast of numbers of new members, or the size of the church or its budget, community prominence, or large youth programs. But these can be deceptive, for as the saying goes, "not all that glitters is gold." What really counts, the true measure of a ministry, may be harder to measure: the spiritual health of a congregation. This is Paul's claim.

In the second part of this chapter, verses 4–7, Paul turns to twin themes of confidence and competence. Again, the Corinthians may be playing Paul off against others who in their judgment exude greater confidence or appear to be more competent at preaching. When Paul responds, he does an odd thing. He doesn't argue that he is really competent. No, neither his competence nor his confidence are things he possesses in himself. Whatever competence or confidence he has are gifts of God. God is the basis of Paul's confidence and strength. His competence comes from God.

The third section of the chapter, verses 7–18, is the longest and most complex. Here Paul argues that what has happened in Jesus Christ is a new thing and such a game-changer that is as if everyone had up until now been under a veil of some sort, one that made everything fuzzy and unclear. But now that veil has been lifted, allowing God to be clearly revealed and allowing Christians direct experience of transformation. To make his point, Paul draws on a story from Exodus 34 about Moses wearing a veil over his face after he had been with God. Moses did this to protect the people from a radiance that they said would be too much for them.

Paul spoke of the difference between the old covenant mediated by Moses and the new covenant in Christ. We need to be careful here lest we make too simple a contrast, and one that Paul is not making, between Judaism and Christianity, as if one were wrong and the other right. The contrast is not so much between the two religions as it is between two ways of being religious or spiritual.

One way, which Paul describes quite bluntly as "the ministry of death" (vs. 7), is a religion that requires human beings to do all sorts of things and to attain a form of perfection in order that they are acceptable to God. This makes religion, whether Judaism or Christianity, a little like earning merit badges. If you get enough of them, then you are "in," and "accepted." But this is not the new covenant or the gospel of Jesus Christ. That gospel says you don't have to do something—or anything—to get on God's good side. So stop, for God's sake, with all your self-centered busyness! What the gospel says to us is that when we couldn't make ourselves acceptable, God did that for us. God took the initiative. You don't have to do anything to get on God's good side, because in Christ God has already taken your side. Trust this and live gratefully.

The famed South African bishop, Desmond Tutu, made a similar point by saying that, despite what many people think, "Christianity is not a religion of virtue." A religion of virtue, said Tutu, "tells us, 'If you are good, then God will love you.' But Christianity is not a religion of virtue, it is a religion of grace. A religion of grace says to us, 'You are loved. You are loved. So then live like beloved and cherished sons and daughters of God." What Tutu calls a religion of virtue is what Paul had experienced as a "ministry of death," asking of him a perfection he could never achieve. But with the new covenant, that is now over and done. The veil has been taken away. You are freed by Christ, by grace given as a gift, for an altogether new kind of life.

LESSON 1 HOMEWORK QUESTIONS

❶ When are letters of reference used in our society? Are they sometimes helpful or even necessary? What are their limits?

❷ Read Exodus 34: 29-35, to which Paul alludes here in Chapter 3. What do you think the Exodus passage is about? How has Paul interpreted it?

❸ Why do you think Paul described the old covenant as a "ministry of death"?

❹ Can you think of experiences in your own life where you didn't feel that you "measured up" or were "worthy"? What's it like to feel you have to keep proving your worth or doing things/ achieving things to prove your value or worthiness to be loved? 5. This passage from 2 Corinthians appears in the lectionary (the church's appointed cycle of readings) on Transfiguration Sunday, when Jesus is said to have glowed with the very power and presence of God. Does this use of the passage make good sense as you see it? Why or why not?

LESSON 1: CLASS SESSION
RESPONSE TIME

Write down responses to the following:

In this passage, a message of God who is still speaking to me is . . .

In this passage, a message of God who is still speaking for our church is . . .

Today I leave with this question. . .

Next week's lesson:
2 Corinthians, Chapter 4:1–15, Earthen Vessels

CLOSING PRAYER
Prayer Concerns:

Notes:

lesson 2

Earthen Vessels

2 CORINTHIANS, CHAPTER 4:1-15

HOMEWORK

STEP ❶: First Reading

Find a comfortable place to sit, when you can be undisturbed for 15 minutes or so. Read the text slowly, prayerfully and meditatively. Savor the words. Pray them. Put yourself into the text with your sense. What do you hear, smell, or feel? Pay attention to the words or phrases that "speak to you," or "jump out at you." Consider reading it aloud.

STEP ❷: Second Reading

This may happen at the same time as the first reading or at a different time or on another day. For this second reading, note any questions you might have. Is the reading all one, or can you see subsections or parts? Who are the main characters? Is there a plot or story? Note additional information you need—place names, monetary values, etc.—to better understand what's going on.

YOUR NOTES:

STEP ❸: Interpreting the Text

In the United Church of Christ's *Book of Worship*, there is a section in the back titled "Comfort from Scripture." It contains words from scripture that the pastor may want to read at bedsides, gravesides and in those moments of despair in people's lives. Part of this powerful text reminds us that we have a treasure in our earthen bodies and that the transcendent power belongs to God, not us. The text is divided into two parts; Paul defends his faithfulness to the Gospel (v.1-6) and claims the hardship of ministry through hope (v.7-15).

Paul is speaking about his own ministry in this passage, and he is on the defensive. He is mindful that he had once persecuted the church and that it had taken the power of God to change him and turn him toward the light. He did not come to ministry through his own efforts or accomplishments, but through the saving action of a merciful God. As a recipient of God's mercy, he can do nothing more or less than be faithful to God's mission. Everything that he is and everything he does is sustained through the power of God's activity in his life.

When accusations are made against him and comparisons are raised, Paul sticks to his guns. He refutes the criticism against him by discussing the state of mind of the unbelievers; they are simply not ready to receive the remarkable light of Christ, the light that changes everything. (Preachers today, take heed!) Unbelief is a natural part of every age and we cannot easily explain it away. It's easy to blame the gods of this world, but in reality, it just may be that the fault lies with those who are preaching it. We must never let ourselves off the hook by explaining unbelief away. We've got to claim the Gospel for ourselves and present it in such a way as to break through to the listener.

Paul refutes the notion that his preaching is too self-referential. Even though he has never taken a preaching class, he knows that the Gospel is not merely a set of ideas and truths without grounding in human experience. He "proclaims Jesus Christ as Lord" and he is Christ's servant. His service to Jesus Christ is shared with the Corinthian community, reminding them that they are also servants for and with each other.

Finally, in this first section of our text, Paul affirms the light that does not come from himself or anyone else. The words flow from him in a shower of praise, "the light of the knowledge of the glory of God in the face of Jesus Christ." Paul is practically overwhelmed by the full-on power of the light and grace that has come to him through the mercy of God. Paul's life was changed forever by that light on the road to Damascus. He knows that nothing less than the transforming power of God's brightness will change the heart of all creation and the human heart.

The second section of the fourth chapter takes up the weighty subject of life made real through sacrifice and, sometimes, death. This is not for the faint of heart, but for all who claim for themselves the life of Jesus in their own skins. The treasure that is held in the clay pot that has the name "Paul" on it contains the light of Christ that he has just referred to a sentence ago. Paul believes that every Christian life is lived most fully when life is given up for the ministry of others and we become living reflections of Jesus' life.

Our human weakness must always be seen as an opportunity for God to work within us. The power of Paul's ministry doesn't spring from him, but from the transcendent power of God that has made a home in his being. By all accounts, Paul should be crushed, driven to despair, forsaken and destroyed because of all he has been through. But it is the power of God that has enabled him to get through all that has been handed him. For some, it would mean that they are tough or stubborn or uncommonly strong; for Paul, it means that God's grace has come to him. God's power has arrived through his own weakness. The mighty power of God is alive in the breath and bones and body of Paul's existence.

Finally we return to a common theme for Paul; Christ has died for or perhaps instead of him. But the one who raised Jesus will also raise us into life again and we will be brought into Christ's presence. All this flows from the amazing grace of God who extends grace to more and more people.

LESSON 2 HOMEWORK QUESTIONS

❶ Paul famously describes us as "earthen vessels" or clay jars. What do these images convey to you about our human experience? How are our lives held by the Creator God?

❷ There were those around Paul who were extremely critical of his ministry and especially of his preaching. As you read the text, do you hear his defense against unbelievers as relevant for today? Do we proclaim Jesus Christ as Lord in ways that an unbeliever might be able to hear and respond to?

❸ There are many hardships and difficulties in the Christian life. Paul reminds us that we can face difficult times by carrying Jesus in our very bodies. Have you had such an experience, a time when you knew that God was with you, holding you and helping you through a difficult time? Did it make a difference to know that God was present with you?

❹ One of the strongest images of the chapter is in v. 6, when Paul suggests that the glory of God shines in the face of Jesus Christ. Have you seen that kind of light reflected in the face of someone you know? Have you witnessed the light shining in the faces of those who are around you? How might the light of Jesus be reflected in your face?

LESSON 2 CLASS SESSION
RESPONSE TIME
Write down responses to the following:

In this passage, a message of God who is still speaking to me is . . .

In this passage, a message of God who is still speaking for our church is . . .

Today I leave with this question. . .

Next week's lesson:
Chapter 5:14–6:2, God's Reconciliation Reach Out

CLOSING PRAYER
Prayer Concerns:

Notes:

lesson 3
God's Reconciliation Reach Out
2 CORINTHIANS 5:14-6: 2

HOMEWORK

STEP ❶: First Reading

Find a comfortable place to sit, when you can be undisturbed for 15 minutes or so. Read the text slowly, prayerfully and meditatively. Savor the words. Pray them. Put yourself into the text with your sense. What do you hear, smell, or feel? Pay attention to the words or phrases that "speak to you," or "jump out at you." Consider reading it aloud.

STEP ❷: Second Reading

This may happen at the same time as the first reading or at a different time or on another day. For this second reading, note any questions you might have. Is the reading all one, or can you see subsections or parts? Who are the main characters? Is there a plot or story? Note additional information you need—place names, monetary values, etc.—to better understand what's going on.

YOUR NOTES:

STEP ❸: Interpreting the Text

This is one of the most famous passages in 2 Corinthians. It is also central to the letter and, really, to Christian faith. As we noted in the background study for Lesson 1, for Paul something has happened in Jesus Christ, something that changes everything.

But what has happened? The key word in this text is "reconciliation." From Paul's perspective, something is broken in the God/ human relationship. We humans have been, as it were, caught—trapped—by the alien powers of Sin and Death as surely as the children of C.S. Lewis's classic, "The Lion, the Witch and the Wardrobe" find a perpetual winter to have Narnia in its grasp.

The power of Sin and Death (capitalized because for Paul sin is not particular misdeeds but a ruling power; same with Death) in our lives and world results in our estrangement from God as well as from one another. We live at odds with God, with others, and with our own selves. In Corinth the evidence of this state of affairs was the factionalism and back-biting in the congregation as well as the Corinthians being in the thrall of slick preachers who spoke of their own great spirituality and power.

Even religion has not helped. It has developed into a system according to which people must do endless things to appease God and try to get on God's good side.

So God must take the initiative to put things right, to effect reconciliation. And that is how Paul describes the meaning of Jesus Christ, his life, death and resurrection. God has acted to change the world, to break the power of Sin and Death and reconcile the world to God, to redeem and reclaim people from Sin and Death's power.

In verse 18 this sequence is very clear. "All this is from God," writes Paul. That is, God takes the initiative to do for us what we cannot do for ourselves. God is the author of this new peace pact. In the second clause of this verse, Paul lays out the means by which God does this . . . "Christ." God "reconciled us to himself through Christ . . . ." Then in the final phrase of this key verse Paul spells out the implication of it all, God entrusts to us, that is, the church, "the message of reconciliation."

Some speak of what God has done in Christ with a doctrine made popular in the Middle Ages: "substitutionary atonement." The way this is often presented is that God was really angry at how sinful human beings were and demanded a sacrifice to put things right. So Jesus had to die as a "substitute" for us. Note how different that doctrine is from what Paul actually says here. Paul doesn't speak of a distant, angry God who must be appeased by a sacrifice. He speaks of a God who takes initiative to reach out to human beings, by becoming human. Christ's death is not about appeasing God's anger, but expressing the depth of God's commitment to God's creation. In Christ's life, ministry, death and resurrection, we see just how far God will go to find us when we are lost and to bring us home again.

For Paul, the result of God's initiative in Christ is to set human beings free from the twin evil powers of Sin and Death, and to effect a whole New Creation (verse 17). But let's note a couple of additional important, possibly surprising, things. This is not just about individuals being forgiven, although it includes that. It is "the world" (verse 19) God has reconciled. The implications are not limited to individuals—it's bigger, cosmic. Nor are the implications for life after death alone. The New Creation (see 6: 1–2) is here and now. And here and now, the church is called to embody reconciliation in the midst of the world.

If all this seems like a lot to grasp (and it is) perhaps we can find an analogy that many today know something about: recovery from addiction. The very influential 12-step recovery program affirms a couple of things that sound very much like what Paul is telling us here. First, we humans have a problem. Our lives are a mess. Two, we can't fix it by ourselves, we need help. Three, we have help—from God, who can do for us what we can't do for ourselves: free us from our compulsive behavior, whether it is bondage to drugs, alcohol, work, food, sex, shopping, pleasing people, etc. As we rely on God's strength for help, we also take responsibility for our own lives and behavior. And, in the world of recovery, newly sober people are to bring the message of hope and healing to others who still suffer.

My point is not that Christianity is just a 12-step program. Rather, these programs do provide a contemporary analogy that may help us understand Paul's message of reconciliation and new creation.

LESSON 3 HOMEWORK QUESTIONS

❶ The word "reconciliation" is a key one here. Look up "reconciliation" in a dictionary. What does it mean? How does what you read fit (or not) with what Paul is talking about here?

❷ In the study section above, "Sin" is described as not just "sins," that is particular misdeeds or failings, but as a power that has human beings in its grip. The same with Death: not so much individual, personal death, but a power that rules by fear. Does this make sense to you? Why or why not?

❸ Can you think of some contemporary examples of people, whether famous or known only to you or a few, who you might describe as "messengers of reconciliation," both in their words and their actions? Describe them.

❹ In the study, 12-step programs like AA are suggested as an analogy to what Paul describes here. Consider talking with someone you know who is active in such a program or attend an open meeting. How do these experiences illuminate this passage for you?

❺ This passage is often read on Ash Wednesday, the day in which the season of Lent begins. Why do you think it is chosen for that day?

LESSON 3 CLASS SESSION
RESPONSE TIME

Write down responses to the following:

In this passage, a message of God who is still speaking to me is . . .

In this passage, a message of God who is still speaking for our church is . . .

Today I leave with this question. . .

Next week's lesson:
2 Corinthians, Chapter 9:1–15, Hilarious Giving

CLOSING PRAYER
Prayer Concerns:

Notes:

lesson 4

Hilarious Giving

2 CORINTHIANS 9:1–15

HOMEWORK

STEP ❶: First Reading

Find a comfortable place to sit, when you can be undisturbed for 15 minutes or so. Read the text slowly, prayerfully and meditatively. Savor the words. Pray them. Put yourself into the text with your sense. What do you hear, smell, or feel? Pay attention to the words or phrases that "speak to you," or "jump out at you." Consider reading it aloud.

STEP ❷: Second Reading

This may happen at the same time as the first reading or at a different time or on another day. For this second reading, note any questions you might have. Is the reading all one, or can you see subsections or parts? Who are the main characters? Is there a plot or story? Note additional information you need—place names, monetary values, etc.—to better understand what's going on.

YOUR NOTES:

STEP ❸: Interpreting the Text

It may come as a surprise to us that amid all the focus of this letter on such big weighty theological matters as the message of the gospel, the nature of authentic ministry and the meaning of leadership in the church, Paul devotes basically two chapters (8 and 9) to a fund drive. But then, as someone observed long ago, "Unless a person's faith affects their pocketbook, it is phony."

This collection for the needs of the poor in the Jerusalem church is understood by Paul as an offering, an offering to God. But there's more. Paul is appealing to churches composed of Gentiles, in Achaia, the region in which Corinth is located, to give generously to support a church composed of Jews in far-off Jerusalem. Therein lies one of the great dramas in the life of the early church, about which you can read much more in the Book of Acts, and Acts Chapter 15 in particular.

The earliest Christians were all Jews. The mother church was in Jerusalem. Paul, however, had been called to cross a huge cultural divide and preach the gospel among the Gentiles (Greeks and Romans). Could the gospel bring together in one church people of two such different cultures? Could the Jewish Christians welcome the Gentile Christians? Could the Gentile Christians raise money for their Jewish Christian counterparts? Think of some of the racial, ethnic and cultural differences in our own time and in the church today. Imagine being asked to raise money for people you don't know, people very different from you, and when there was surely plenty of need "right here, at home." It is pretty clear that Paul is trying to build the bonds between people who had been separated and mutually suspicious. In that sense, the rubber meets the road, here, for the ministry of reconciliation discussed in the previous Lesson.

Paul employs a number of strategies to encourage the Corinthians to give generously. One of them is competition. He calls to the attention of the Corinthians the generous giving of the church to their north, in Macedonia. Call it "keeping up with the Macedonians." Perhaps this seems tacky to us? In some churches, giving is supposed to be very hush-hush and private. The difficulty with that is that it deprives us of the inspiring examples of others' generosity. I, for one, have been moved to a higher level of generosity by hearing the testimony of other people about their giving. Maybe privacy and secrecy are over-rated?

But the larger focus here might be thought of as "getting into the flow," the flow of generosity. God has given generously, extravagantly to us (9: 15) in many ways, chief among them Christ Jesus. The Corinthians are invited to join this flow of generosity and to express it with some generous giving of their own. Paul reminds the Corinthians how it works: "The one who sows sparingly will also reap sparingly, and the one who sows bountifully, will also reap bountifully." The idea here is that in giving we receive. It may not make sense from a cold, hard rational point of view, but that doesn't mean it's not true. Though it may defy common sense, generosity does seem to enrich those who practice it.

In verse 7 Paul writes an oft-quoted line: "God loves a cheerful giver." Paul doesn't just want the Corinthians to give, he wants them to be happy about it! The Greek word that is translated as "cheerful," is *hilarion* from which come the English words "hilarious," and "hilarity." Imagine a "hilarious giver."

One Sunday the speaker in our adult education program was a hospice nurse. She told a story about helping an older woman come home from the hospital. Home to die. After she got the woman settled, the nurse noticed a bottle of the expensive "My Sin" perfume on her dresser. She asked, "Dear, before I go, would you like me to dab a little perfume behind your ears?" The older woman replied, "Honey, why don't you just splash it on!"

That evening I called on a family as part of the annual stewardship program. We talked with one another about money and faith and shared about our pledges for the coming year. The pledge of this family was very large, so large that I was shocked. My cool, rational self asked, "Are you really okay with that?" The couple said, "Well, we heard that nurse this morning, what she said about 'Splash it on.' We've been fortunate. We decided we wanted to 'Splash it on.'" I headed home that night amazed by what God can do.

LESSON 4 HOMEWORK QUESTIONS

❶ If your Bible has maps in the back, locate Corinth, the region of Achaia, and the region of Macedonia. (If your Bible does not have maps, search online or look in the library for a Bible Atlas.) Now find Jerusalem. What significance do you find in this map study?

❷ In verse 12 of chapter 9, Paul indicates that this offering will serve two purposes. What are they?

❸ What other congregations is your church connected to and how? Is it important, do you think, to be connected to other churches? Why?

❹ Paul tells us in several places (verses 8 and 10) that God blesses us as we bless others. Can you think of an experience of this in your life?

❺ Is there a difference between a "fund-drive" and an "offering"? If so, how would you describe the difference?

LESSON 4: CLASS SESSION
RESPONSE TIME

Write down responses to the following:

In this passage, a message of God who is still speaking to me is . . .

In this passage, a message of God who is still speaking for our church is . . .

Today I leave with this question. . .

Next week's lesson:

2 Corinthians 11:1–15, Taking on False Apostles

CLOSING PRAYER

Prayer Concerns:

Notes:

lesson 5
Taking on False Apostles
2 CORINTHIANS 11:1–15

HOMEWORK

STEP ❶: First Reading

Find a comfortable place to sit, when you can be undisturbed for 15 minutes or so. Read the text slowly, prayerfully and meditatively. Savor the words. Pray them. Put yourself into the text with your sense. What do you hear, smell, or feel? Pay attention to the words or phrases that "speak to you," or "jump out at you." Consider reading it aloud.

STEP ❷: Second Reading

This may happen at the same time as the first reading or at a different time or on another day. For this second reading, note any questions you might have. Is the reading all one, or can you see subsections or parts? Who are the main characters? Is there a plot or story? Note additional information you need—place names, monetary values, etc.—to better understand what's going on.

YOUR NOTES:

STEP ❸: Interpreting the Text

Paul is about to depart into dangerous territory as he seeks to defend, not only himself, but his understanding of the Gospel, to the Corinthians who are attracted to other apostles and other forms of the Gospel. He is unaccustomed to bragging, but the situation at Corinth has become so intense that he has to haul out his achievements and boast about his ministry. Paul begs them to put up with his foolish ways because he knows that he has got to pull out all the stops for the Gospel. He knows he is in risky territory, so he wants to disarm his listeners.

Of course, he loves the folks at Corinth, who responded to his ministry with a spirit of love and devotion. He compares himself to a father presenting his daughter to her husband in marriage. He fears that they will be led astray by outsiders, just as Eve was put out of the Garden by the serpent. Paul fears the worst: will his people be entranced by another way of interpreting Jesus or a different Spirit than the one that he taught? Paul is both worried and secure, walking a thin line between telling the Corinthians that they are following the wrong path and desiring to compete with the "super-apostles" who have threatened his ministry.

As usual, Paul brings up his sense of inferiority. He realizes he is not the greatest elocutionist, but he holds to the strength and power of his message. Once again, he reminds his readers that he possesses the knowledge of God and that is by far the most important aspect of his ministry and his message. Paul's superiority lies in the fact that he has knowledge of God. He doesn't say so directly, but implies that it is not so true for others.

Next, (v.7–11) Paul enters into a discussion about the financial cost of presenting the Gospel. He reminds folks that he was not an expensive minister; it cost them nothing to have him establish a new church. He wanted financial freedom in order to evangelize communities in the way he thought was best. He didn't want to be beholden to others, so he practiced a trade and kept his independence. By doing so, Paul contends that the Gospel flourishes through freedom and love.

His opponents have been claiming the same principles, but they are accepting money and not being transparent about it (v.12-15). Paul is on to them! He exposes them for who he believes them to be: deceivers, masquerading as apostles, a sorry bunch of crooks. He goes so far as to name them as Satan's workers, a charge that he levels with alarming certainty. Satan passes as someone who is good, but actually is evil and deceitful. He charmed Eve and passed himself off as an angel of light. Paul holds nothing back. He so dislikes and disdains his rivals that he must speak the truth to their power in plain and bold terms.

For Paul, everything he has worked toward is at stake and he will not back down. For those who are the enemies of Christ, their end will be what they deserve. God will have the last laugh and the last judgment. They have performed Satan's work and to Satan they will finally go.

LESSON 5 HOMEWORK QUESTIONS

❶ Paul describes his position with the Church at Corinth as "folly" or foolish. He even describes himself as a fool for Christ. How might Paul's foolishness be a wise move in relationship to the situation at Corinth?

❷ The Church is being led down a path that is not conducive to the Gospel as Paul knows it in Jesus Christ. He believes that the deception is corrupt and destructive for the Corinthians and the Church. He wants the Church to return to "the real Christ" and away from an outward show. There are many "Jesus Shows" in our culture today. How can we be sure of "the real Christ"?

❸ Paul contrasts himself with his rivals with regard to his speaking ability. "I may not be a trained speaker," he writes, "but I do have knowledge." Do we place a stronger emphasis on oratorical skill than we do on our intellectual grasp of the Gospel?

❹ Paul insisted on preaching the Gospel free of charge. His critics claimed that he did so because he simply wasn't a great preacher. But Paul was clear that he wanted the Gospel to be free of charge. How does his message line up with today's stewardship and evangelism pitches?

❺ The language Paul uses against his rivals is harsh and uncompromising. Paul uses terms that we might hesitate before using in our religious circles today for fear of sounding intolerant and unreasonable. Are there any situations and activities that require such judgment?

LESSON 5: CLASS SESSION
RESPONSE TIME

Write down responses to the following:

In this passage, a message of God who is still speaking to me is . . .

In this passage, a message of God who is still speaking for our church is . . .

Today I leave with this question. . .

Next week's lesson:
2 Corinthians 11:16–12:13, Playing the Fool

CLOSING PRAYER
Prayer Concerns:

Notes:

I told the mountain to move

by Phillis Rayburn.

lesson 6

Playing the Fool
2 CORINTHIANS 11:16–12:13

HOMEWORK

STEP ❶: First Reading

Find a comfortable place to sit, when you can be undisturbed for 15 minutes or so. Read the text slowly, prayerfully and meditatively. Savor the words. Pray them. Put yourself into the text with your sense. What do you hear, smell, or feel? Pay attention to the words or phrases that "speak to you," or "jump out at you." Consider reading it aloud.

STEP ❷: Second Reading

This may happen at the same time as the first reading or at a different time or on another day. For this second reading, note any questions you might have. Is the reading all one, or can you see subsections or parts? Who are the main characters? Is there a plot or story? Note additional information you need—place names, monetary values, etc.—to better understand what's going on.

YOUR NOTES:

STEP ❸: Interpreting the Text

There are few things that annoy us more than braggarts. They can break up a good dinner party or drive us crazy if we get stuck next to them on a plane, simply by talking too much about themselves. Paul has done a fair amount of bragging in the final chapters of his second letter to the Corinthians, so we must try to understand where he is coming from and why he would risk alienating his readers by boasting about his accomplishments. At least he realized he was bragging and saw clearly the foolishness of comparing himself with others. Without this self-awareness, we might easily dismiss Paul as just another self-preoccupied preacher more concerned with elevating himself than proclaiming the Gospel.

The reason for all this self-commendation is that his opponents have made claims about their superiority and Paul will not allow them to win without a great fight. His own abilities are equal to theirs, if not better, and so he justifies his need to boast (11:16–21a) and then does so in three different ways. He describes his general mission activity (11:21b–29), a terribly humiliating experience (11:30–33), and a vision, through which he learned a great lesson (12:1–10). Finally, he returns to the theme of boasting in order to ask for forgiveness (12:11–13).

For Paul, boasting is plain foolishness; the only reason for boasting at all is to brag about Christ. He actually doesn't view himself as a fool, but rather as a disciple of Christ, called to play the fool for Christ. There is an ironic quality to his writing; he worries that he may appear as a clown, but he is willing to do anything in order to make the Gospel central in the lives of others. He also worries that his authority will be undercut by his methodology, and hopes that God desires the ultimate outcome and will support his foolishness for the sake of the Gospel.

So he continues to brag. His opponents have been boasting all along, but he is sure he will come out on top, even though he resents having to go this way. He is a Hebrew, just like them; he is Jewish to the core and now goes at them for their relationship to Christ. It's his ace in the hole. He has been imprisoned, beaten, tossed at sea and faced danger too many times to mention. The list of suffering is long and hard-won, but Paul is more concerned about his ministry than his suffering. Sounding like a parish pastor or area minister, he names the spiritual stress of concern for all the churches as his biggest worry. There is no greater suffering than the anxiety of worrying over the flock and he has done plenty of it. Paul embraces the power of his own spiritual strength and the weakness of congregations without him.

He now describes three experiences that point to his life in Christ. The first was at Damascus. The King, who wanted to capture and most likely kill him, hunted him down. He had to be lowered in a basket through a window in the city wall. He felt humiliated and cowardly as he snuck out of town. But he would gladly suffer this humiliation for the sake of the Gospel.

As Chapter 12 begins, Paul moves on to describe the second experience as a powerful vision and revelation. It is so personal that he has held on to it for all these years, but now feels compelled to speak, even though the experience goes "beyond words." He was taken up in the third heaven or Paradise. The third heaven is the highest heaven and may actually have represented life after death. The revelation remains mysterious to him, and he tells the story as if it happened to another. But he knew and we know; it happened to him. Again, he does not want to brag about it, but he needs to communicate his credentials as a receiver of revelations.

Last, he confesses that he simply should not be making claims about these extraordinary experiences; he would rather embrace his own weakness. All the suffering and the weaknesses he has been bragging about have been because of the cross. Now he introduces two phrases, "thorn in the flesh" and the "messenger of Satan," as another witness to his weakness.

We are not sure what these phrases imply, but there has been plenty of good guessing— perhaps a bodily ailment such as epilepsy, a speech impediment or a weak limb. It could be a mental issue such as depression or despair or even impatience. Whatever it was, Paul has prayed for its removal more than once—he states that he prayed three times.

The lesson Paul learned is a big one: "My grace is sufficient for you, my power is made perfect in weakness." Paul grasps the understanding that God's power overwhelms our human condition and invokes our acceptance of God's amazing grace. One of the paradoxes of the Christian journey is that our human weakness invites us to seek the strength of God. Paul's "thorn" moved him to seek God. Human weakness invokes strength, not our own, but God's.

It is easy for us to be turned off to the fair amount of bragging that is part of the end of this letter. Paul believed he had to play his life up to the Corinthians in self-defense, not only of his ministry but for the sake of the Gospel. He knows that he is playing the fool in a fool's game. Through his self-awareness and his willingness to cling to the cross of Christ, however, we are given a window into his spirit and his faith. He saw that his boasting was a fool's game he was required to play to further his ministry. In his remarkable weakness, we see the strength and grace of God shining through.

LESSON 6 HOMEWORK QUESTIONS

❶ Our culture is one of self-promotion, and a fair amount of self-importance seems to be quite normal. Paul boasts a fair amount in our text. How comfortable are you with bragging?

❷ The image of a fool is utilized in order to discuss Paul's accomplishments. He contrasts it with wisdom. What is wise and what is foolishness for you?

❸ Paul shares three ways in which his experience empowered him as a Christian. He boasts about one, but also says it was humiliating. Can you think of an experience in which you were both humbled and filled with pride?

❹ Do you believe in revelations and visions? Can you think of a dream or vision in which you were captivated by an image of heaven or another life?

❺ The phrase "My grace is sufficient for you, for my power is made perfect in weakness" has been spoken at hospital bedsides and in the midst of an especially difficult time in a Christian's life. Does this verse resonate with your experience? When we are at our weakest, are we strong enough to see God's grace?

LESSON 6: CLASS SESSION
RESPONSE TIME

Write down responses to the following:

In this passage, a message of God who is still speaking to me is . . .

In this passage, a message of God who is still speaking for our church is . . .

Today I leave with this question. . .

CLOSING PRAYER
Prayer Concerns:

Notes:

leader's guide
The Leader's Role & Life Together in Your Bible Study Group

The leader plays a crucial role in keeping the group on task and focused. This is the primary role of the leader. The leader does not need to be an expert on the Bible or on 2 Corinthians. He or she does need to be comfortable leading a group with a strong but gentle hand. It will be important that the leader pay close attention to both the Scripture lesson itself and to the interpretative material in the lesson plan. She or he will need to be prepared to summarize, if possible in his or her own words, the key themes. If putting the material in one's own words is a bit more of a challenge than you as a leader are ready for, you may simply read to the group the key themes material.

The leader is also charged with keeping the group itself moving through the steps of the format and design. One person may lead all six sessions, or the role of leader may move among different members of the group. Either way, the role is important. The leader needs to come well prepared and be comfortable guiding the group's process. *Successful classes and study groups do not wander all over the place, nor are group members who may be inclined to "take over" allowed to do so.*

To keep the group and experience focused the leader is encouraged to clearly state the group purpose at the beginning of each session.

Purpose Statement:

The purpose of this class is to study 2 Corinthians and by doing so to grow in our knowledge and understanding of Scripture, to hear God's word for us and for our church today, and to grow in our friendship with one another.

To make the experience most fruitful, group members are also encouraged to come prepared, having done their homework!

To support the group and the leader, we include a group "Covenant" that expresses group norms. We encourage you to review and re-affirm this covenant at the beginning of each session. (See "Class Session Outline" below).

Timing and Options

Lessons have been planned for congregations that have a 50-minute time period on Sunday morning. But lessons can be expanded to 90 minutes by allowing more time for discussion and sharing. If you are able to expand the time, we encourage you to also enlarge the prayer experience at the conclusion of each lesson. Instead of simply having a closing prayer, the leader may invite people in the groups to share their own prayer concerns before a time of prayer. Leaders may also encourage class members to write down these shared prayer concerns and to hold in prayer during the week the concerns and people who have shared them. This format of sharing prayer concerns can also be done during the 50-minute framework, providing concerns are kept brief. We encourage you to consider enriching the prayer experience in this way.

Beyond this option, leaders may adapt this material and the lesson plans to their group and setting. For example, some leaders may wish to draw on the "Interpreting the Text" commentary and homework questions for the group session itself. We want to provide a clear structure that you can rely on, but we also want leaders and groups to adapt this material in ways that work best for you where you are.

Overview of Lesson and Flow of Classes

Each lesson has two parts, the Homework and the Class Session. The Homework consists of four parts. Each class session consists of ten steps. Here they are in outline:

Homework

❶ First reading of the biblical passage

❷ Second reading of biblical passage

❸ "Interpreting the Text" commentary

❹ Homework questions

Class Session

❶ Welcome all, introductions and nametags as needed

❷ Review of Class Purpose and Class Covenant

❸ Opening prayer

❹ Reading the biblical passage aloud (a silent, individual re-reading following the out-loud reading is an option)

❺ Participant sharing of words or phrases from lesson. Note: this out-loud sharing need not be full sentences, only the words or phrases from the lesson that struck people, that touched or provoked them as they listened. At this point, there is to be neither discussion or crosstalk (things like, "I don't agree," or giving advice, e.g. "oh yeah, I had that concern once," " or "what you need to do is . . . ."

❻ Leader's Presentation

❼ Group discussion guided by leader questions

❽ Response Time, writing brief responses to three questions

❾ Sharing, as people wish, of what they wrote. Again, at this point there is no discussion or crosstalk, only listening to one another.

❿ Reminder of next week's lesson and closing prayer

And now . . . have fun! Listen for the Spirit! Enjoy 2 Corinthians!

Class Session Outline

Use this outline for each class session. Following the outline, you will find a **Leader's Presentation and Questions for Discussion** for each of the six lessons.

Welcome All (Welcome through sharing first responses, 15 minutes)

Invite people to share names or wear name tags.

Review of Purpose and Our Covenant

Class may develop its own purpose and covenant or use the following. These should be read/stated at each session. The leader should read the Purpose Statement out loud and then the class should affirm the Covenant by reading it aloud together.

Purpose Statement

The purpose of this class is to study 2 Corinthians and by doing so to grow in our knowledge and understanding of Scripture, to hear God's word for us and for our church today, and to grow in our friendship with one another.

Our Covenant

We covenant to be present and on time each week (unless excused by speaking with the class leader beforehand).

We covenant to prepare our homework faithfully.

We covenant to participate in each class session fully and to support others in their full participation.

We covenant to participate in ways that are respectful of all participants and to the leader.

If we have concerns or suggestions about our class, we covenant to share those directly with our class leader(s).

Opening Prayer

Read text aloud

Silent re-reading (optional) followed by sharing (3–5 minutes)

Leader invites participants to share words or phrases from the reading that struck them, that touched, disturbed or excited them. This is done without crosstalk or discussion, simply hearing and acknowledging.

Leader's Presentation (5–7 minutes)

The leader should review "Interpreting the Text" and "Leader's Presentation and Questions for Group Discussion" for the current lesson, then speak briefly in their own words about the passage. Alternately, the leader may simply read the "Leader's Presentation," or part of it, to the group.

Group Discussion (15 minutes)

Explore several of the themes that are most important to you.

Response Time (3 minutes)

Ask the participants to use pen and paper to complete the following sentences:

In this passage, a message of God who is stilling speaking to me is . . .

In this passage, a message of God who is still speaking for our church is . . .

Today I leave with this question . . .

Invite sharing of responses without discussion or debate (5 minutes).

Thank participants, note next week's lesson, offer closing prayer.

Lesson 1: Leader's Presentation & Questions for Discussion

The Great Unveiling

2 CORINTHIANS 3:1–18.

The leader should review Interpreting the Text, and the following key themes, to talk about, in your own words, 2 Corinthians 3:1–18.

As noted in "Interpreting the Text," this chapter of Paul's letter is not exactly straight-forward or easy to grasp! In the context of the letter, he seems to be making at least two points.

One point is to contrast the way Paul presents and validates his ministry in contrast to that of others—others by whom the Corinthians seem considerably more impressed. These others have lots of letters of reference, glowing reports, endorsements from influential people. Think of the lines in movie reviews or on book covers telling you this is "a must-see" or "a book that will change your life."

Paul says the gospel has changed the game. It's no longer about having credentials or accolades comparable to other rock-star orators of the time. What Paul cares about is the kind of lives produced in others by his preaching and teaching. Are these lives faithful, mature, and spiritually healthy?

The second point builds on the first. The game has been changed. It's not about our achievements or our connections. It's not about who we know. It's not about having a whole list of achievements or accomplishments that show God or people that we are valuable or loved or important. That, Paul says, is a spirit-killing rat race. Something new has happened in Christ. Namely, when we were trapped in that rat race, trapped in fear and sin, God came to us in Christ to set us free. God entered into life as we know it to free us and bring us home to God as God's beloved. And because of this everything is changed. The gauzy veils that clouded our minds have been torn away so that we can see clearly.

The discussion might focus on the contrast mentioned in "Interpreting the Text" between a "religion of virtue" and a "religion of grace." What's your experience of Christianity and the church? Is it more a religion of virtue as Tutu defines it? Or a religion of grace? Where have you experienced real grace—a gift of love and acceptance—in your life? What have been the consequences of grace in your life? Might the experience of grace be described as something like the "lifting of a veil"?

Notes:

Lesson 2: Leader's Presentation & Questions for Discussion

Earthen Vessels

2 CORINTHIANS 4:1–15

The leader should review Interpreting the Text, and the following key themes, to talk about, in your own words, 2 Corinthians 4:1–15.

For those who are curious about the struggles of ministry, this chapter provides a powerful description, not only of what it means to be a minister of the gospel, but of the struggles and hardships of the call. Paul is remarkably clear-eyed throughout; he did not obtain his ministry on his own, but through the mercy of God. God's mercy serves all of us, no matter if we serve as pastors of persons. We are sustained in our calling through the mercy of God.

Paul is on the defensive about his ministry once again, but he presents a clear case for the Gospel's power to change lives rather than relying on the star-studded preachers of the time. Paul's life has been turned around through a direct experience of the light; he knows first-hand what can happen when a life is changed and charged with the power of a transforming God. It may seem that he dwells on the negative and is even overly defensive, but Paul is full of faith in God and overwhelmed by the power of Christ.

The phrase "the light of the knowledge of the glory of God shining in the face of Jesus Christ" reminds us that the Gospel is capable of chasing away darkness and hardship, compelling us to embrace the light of the new creation. Paul's witness, even in difficult moments, is unshakable.

Paul continues to describe the pressures of ministry and reminds us that even in those terrible moments, we are not lost because of God's power to help us endure. Even in weakness, God's power is present. Troubles are real, but the power of God helps us to transcend even those times when we might feel that all is lost.

Paul's theology is grounded in the experience of Jesus' own life: we are always carrying in us death, so that life might be realized. Paul lives every day with life and death before him. This is the way of the cross, but it is also the road to life itself.

The discussion could contrast the ways of living with the example of Jesus' life and death before us in our day to day existence. What are the hardships we face each day and how does our faith help us, not only to cope, but at times to transcend our difficulties? Paul is clear that Jesus' life provides the blueprint for grace, mercy and strength.

Notes:

Lesson 3: Leader's Presentation & Questions for Discussion

God's Reconciliation Reach Out

2 CORINTHIANS 5:14–6:2

The leader should review Interpreting the Text, and the following key themes, to talk about, in your own words, 2 Corinthians 5:14–6:2.

This really is a very important and very powerful passage, arguably at the center of the Christian faith and teaching. So leaders will want to prepare carefully and keep their presentation and discussion focused.

Your presentation might start by noting that the message here is not first of all about things we human beings, or Christians, need to do, or believe or feel. It is first of all about what God has done and is doing. Faced with a break-up between God and creation, between God and human beings, God took the initiative. God reached out to us to make peace and a new beginning.

God's means for this "Reconciliation Reach Out" was Christ—his birth, life, teachings, but most of all his death and resurrection. By means of Christ, God went to the very deepest and darkest depths of human experience to find lost human beings and bring us back into a new, restored and healthy relationship with God, with others, and with ourselves.

Many people will have heard all this described through the popular doctrine of the "substitutionary atonement." But Paul is saying something different here. You might discuss the differences (review the "Interpreting the Text" section for this lesson). For some, the analogy of the 12-step movement, AA, or Recovery may prove a helpful way of getting into this. Probably the most challenging element of this for many strong and successful people is the idea that they need help, that they can't do it all by themselves, but they—like everyone else—need help, need grace.

Then there are the implications of God's "Reconciliation Reach Out." What are they? Well, for the Corinthians, Paul asks that they respond to what God has done and start acting like forgiven, freed, healed, loved, redeemed and reconciled people in their life together. This is what prompts Paul to urge in 6:1 that the Corinthians not "accept the grace of God in vain." To accept that message in vain would mean accepting forgiveness, but having it make no difference in our lives or how we treat others.

And second, they—the church—are to embody this message of reconciliation to others. That may mean giving a message to others in words about God. But it may also mean giving a message by the way we live and the way we are a community of people together.

Notes:

Lesson 4: Leader's Presentation & Questions for Discussion

Hilarious Giving

2 CORINTHIANS 9:1–15

The leader should review Interpreting the Text, and the following key themes, to talk about, in your own words, 2 Corinthians 9:1–15

There are a number of different themes and points of reflection/ discussion here. One is simply that the subject of money is raised. Sometimes people want to draw a hard line between the spiritual world and the material world, between spiritual experience and money. Neither the Bible nor Paul really support such a compartmentalization or separation. For Scripture, faith has "on the ground" implications, which includes how we use money and giving.

One of the things Paul consistently does in I and 2 Corinthians is to think theologically about the church and all aspects of it. In other words, he relates whatever he writes about to God, to who God is and what God has done. As we ponder this chapter on the offering for the poor in Jerusalem, how does Paul "think theologically" about this? What does it all have to do with God? Sometimes, in the church, our "fund-raising" efforts don't seem all that different from any other charitable organization. How might Paul help us to frame fund-raising in terms of faith?

Another way to put this is to say that Paul draws out, here, the implications of generosity for a person's spiritual life and health. What are those implications as he sees them?

Yet another theme of this passage, albeit an underlying one, is how in the world do you unify a church that is made up of people of quite different races, cultures, even languages? In this case, those two very different cultures are Jew and Gentile. It's probably difficult for us to appreciate just how different those two worlds were. But perhaps we do know something about bringing people together whose backgrounds and experiences are quite different. Maybe the experience of a blended family is one example that someone in the group will have had? What have people learned about bringing together and building relationship and trust between people who are quite different?

Notes:

Lesson 5: Leader's Presentation & Questions for Discussion

Taking on False Apostles

2 CORINTHIANS 11:1–15

The leader should review Interpreting the Text, and the following key themes, to talk about, in your own words, 2 Corinthians 11:1–15.

Because 2 Corinthians is so concerned with the internal life of the community, we have an insider's view of Paul and his personal response to the struggles and strains of ministry. We meet the man in this text, not the legend, and we witness his pastoral struggles as the founding minister of a new church. If in this chapter we perceive him as personally boastful and highly critical of other leaders, it is because he believes that the situation at Corinth demands it. Are there leaders you know who are self-promoting? Does it turn you off? Are there situations in which the church requires strong, confidant leadership?

Paul's converts are being led by those who he perceives are false apostles and he is concerned for the spiritual welfare of the people. If it sounds like he is bragging, he feels pushed into self-praise and defensiveness by those who have already made significant progress in establishing their brand of ministry at Corinth. In order to combat those powerful forces, Paul must be both wise and foolish. He plays the fool, but with strength and cunning. He is not easily cowed and he will not let the Church go without a good fight.

There is much in this chapter for us today. Paul may not be the most polished and brilliant of speakers, but he believes that the knowledge he possesses is true and reflective of God's purposes. But the Corinthians are caught up in the outward form of gospel success and have lost sight of what is truly important. What is important for the church today? We are surrounded by prosperity gospels on one hand and the threat of the demise of the mainline churches on the other. What does it mean for us to seek true knowledge? How do we evaluate what is most important to us? What is Paul's bottom line?

Paul maintains a policy of offering the Gospel free of charge. He is known as a tent-making pastor, one who makes his living by another craft, so that he has greater freedom to move in the direction that God is leading. Paul did not want to find himself in a situation where the church went one way while God was heading in another. But he also states that he is doing so out of his deep love for the church. The Corinthians have such a unique and special place in his heart, he wants to serve them no matter the cost. When does money "talk" in our congregations? Is there a conflict between money and leadership?

Finally, Paul labels his opponents and takes them on as servants of Satan. This is strong language and some of the harshest words that Paul has written to anyone. There is much at stake here and Paul names it, claims it and refuses to hold back. Can you imagine the threat he must have felt for the sake of the Gospel and his willingness to put so much on the line? The charge is serious. If those false apostles who are coming to Corinth are Satan's servants, then they are not only Paul's opponents, they are enemies of Christ. It is difficult for us to label our enemies today, especially when it comes to other churches and communities of faith. When is it appropriate for us to name the false apostles of our day? What kind of language should we use to address the moral and ethical issues of others?

Notes:

Lesson 6: Leader's Presentation & Questions for Discussion

Playing the Fool

2 CORINTHIANS 11:16–12:13

The leader should review Interpreting the Text, and the following key themes, to talk about, in your own words, 2 Corinthians 11:16–12:13

2 Corinthians places us inside the church and attempts to anchor the church in the Gospel. Although it is written to a particular people in a particular time, the message is not limited to the church at Corinth. Paul is at his best when he describes his commitment to his pastoral responsibilities; he is eloquent, dedicated and he will do anything, including outrageous bragging, to lead his people into a deeper understanding of their faith and the church as the visible Body of Christ in the world.

This letter and in particular this section is not easy to grasp as Paul attempts to describe and defend his ministry in contrast to others. He writes in a way that could offend some folks—he boasts and compares himself to playing the fool. He employs a fair amount of bragging as he discusses his credentials, leaving his readers at times a bit overwhelmed by all that he is willing to do to claim his authority. Everything he has ever done, including some things he will not discuss, is for the sake of the Gospel and good of God's people.

Nevertheless, we are drawn in by Paul's sense of pastoral responsibility and we learn much more about Paul himself than in any other letter. We can see the kind of person he was and we learn about the terrible strains that were placed upon him. We have a sense of his struggle, not only as a pastor and preacher, but as a human being.

Paul also develops a pastoral theology through his letters; he defines for generations the meaning of being a Christian. He describes God's strength and our human weakness in such a way that we can hold on to the assurance, "My grace is sufficient for you, my power is made perfect in weakness."

This is the last session of your 2 Corinthians Bible Study. Thank all participants and note that this is the concluding lesson. As leader, you may wish to provide a brief verbal time of evaluation during the session, or a written form that participants may take and complete at a different time, or both. For a sample evaluation, see next page.

Notes:

Sample Evaluation

❶ What was the most valuable aspect or part of this class for you?

❷ Did you find the material, the study resources, to be helpful?

❸ What comments do you have on the format of classes and their flow?

❹ Comment on your own participation. Did you do the homework? How faithfully did you keep the covenant? How did you engage the material and the group?

❺ What suggestions or additional comments would you offer about this class experience?

Notes: